HOW TO RETIRE EARLY IN MALAYSIA

Get Great Healthcare and Financial Independence

Lisa Reinke

Cover photo licensed 9/25/20 with purchase #193979746 by user
ID 40193562 Lisa Reinke through:
Depositphotos Inc.
Address: 115 West 30th Street, Suite 1110B, New York, NY,
10001, United States
E-mail: support@depositphotos.com
Website: www.depositphotos.com
Phone: +1-954-990-0075 Photo copyright held by Olga Saliy.

Contact the author at author@cheerful.com

ISBN: 9798690375188
Imprint: Independently published

CONTENTS

INTRODUCTION

If you ask any adult about their ultimate dreams when it comes to their professional goals, the majority will say it is to make enough money to retire early. The corporate grind is quickly losing its initial appeal as many young adults are realizing that there is more to life than titles and social status. A decade ago, it was commonplace to brag about how late you stay at work or how few vacation days you take every year. Somehow this distorted image of "busy" life was what teenagers aspired to have. Luckily, after hearing tons of stories from the world's most influential people about how flawed this model of glorifying work above everything else is, people have started to take notice. However, seeking that coveted work-life balance is akin to chasing a mirage that seems to be too good to be true. In truth, as long as you are still in your working years, you have to accept that all you can do is juggle all aspects of your life as best you can. This brings us to early retirement, which is what you should be focusing on instead of unrealistically trying to have the best of both worlds. Retirement has been associated with the elderly for so long that younger generations rarely give it the attention and planning it deserves. Even when they do, they don't use their imagination to contemplate relocating to a place where they can actually enjoy a lifestyle they could only dream of at home. And that is exactly what this book will help you with.

Throughout this book, we will take you on a journey far east to the Southeast Asian country of Malaysia. Known for its mesmerizing beaches and cosmopolitan population, Malaysia is one of the best destinations for your early retirement plans. We will introduce you to the Malaysian culture and let you in on the secrets of guaranteeing yourself great healthcare and financial independence in this beautiful land. After reading this book, you will have a thorough step-by-step guide to begin planning your retirement journey. If you are wondering when you should start, well, the answer is right now. If you want to have a shot at living a comfortable life as an early retiree, you need to start planning today. In the opening chapter, we will get you acquainted with Malaysia and discuss the many reasons why this country deserves to be your retirement destination. Next, in Chapter 2, you will learn about the available healthcare options in Malaysia and how to find one that best suits your needs. In Chapter 3, we will give you ideas on how you can manage your personal finances and enjoy financial independence during your time in Malaysia. Chapter 4 will include some valuable insights and important factors to consider before moving to Malaysia. We then wrap it up in Chapter 5 with a list of actionable items that you can start with today to ensure a smooth transition to Malaysia. Finally, we will close off this book by highlighting the key points that we have discussed throughout. Now that you know what to expect, let's get started!

WHY MALAYSIA?

For years, Malaysia has been among the favored destinations for vacationers from everywhere around the world. Like many Asian countries, Malaysia offers the perfect blend of lush greenery and lively modernism with its tall skyscrapers and bustling city life. This makes it the perfect place for a young retiree who still needs access to both worlds. You can find multiple sources on what to do in Malaysia as a visitor. However, in this chapter, we will be introducing Malaysia in a new light as a place you can call home. What you should expect, and the pros of moving to Malaysia as a retiree, are all important information that can help you see why it's the right place for you and your family.

As an ex-pat, you will appreciate the fact that a little more than half of Malaysia's population is comprised of ex-pats from all over the world. Ranking high on the list of most expat-friendly cities, the capital Kuala Lumpur has the highest percentage of expatriates compared to other Malaysian cities. The city of Penang comes next thanks to its reputation as the Silicon Valley of the East, making it a desirable location for many foreigners. Also, with its relatively lower living costs, Johor is another city that has a great ex-pat community in Malaysia. When looking for a new country to move to, you need to make sure that you find a place where you don't feel so far away from home. This will help you settle faster and facilitate your integration into your new life. It's easier to build a life around a community of like-minded and relatable people.

What Malaysia Has to Offer

Here are some of the benefits that you can expect to enjoy when you retire in Malaysia:

• More Value for Money

When compared to large American and European cities, Malaysia offers a higher value for money in terms of luxuries. For the same amount of money that you would pay in Europe for an average-sized 2-bedroom apartment, you can afford a nice house in one of the most affluent neighborhoods of Malaysia. This is perhaps one of the biggest advantages for a retiree who plans to live off their savings. You want to get more bang for your buck without compromising on the lifestyle that you wish to live. In 2020, the cost of living in Malaysia is 46% lower than in the United States. The cost of rent is on average 74% lower. That's a huge savings.

• Excellent Healthcare System

We will discuss this more in-depth in Chapter 2. However, it's important to note that the Malaysian healthcare system is far more advanced than you would think. Thanks to great public investments, the healthcare system in Malaysia can be compared with that of Western European countries.

• Friendly Nation

Malaysian people are known for their kindness and friendliness. They are used to having foreigners in their country and know how to make them feel welcome. If you are planning on relocating, you will appreciate the fact that you can count on the Malaysians' warmth to make you feel at home even when you are thousands of miles away.

• Beautiful Weather and Scenery

Who wouldn't want to live in a place where the sun is always shining and be surrounded by beautiful landscapes? Living in Malaysia will make you feel like you are on a vacation that never ends. Forget the long dreary winter months back home; the weather in Malaysia is always superb and comfortably predictable.

• Wide Variety of Leisurely Activities

Since you are considering early retirement, it's safe to expect that you are looking forward to having time for life's pleasures. In Malaysia, it's almost impossible to get bored. Whether you are an outdoor adventurer or more into the lavish nightlife, you are bound to find what you want in Malaysia. You will have the chance to explore a new hiking trail every week or even go island hopping in Southeast Asia.

• The Chance to Discover Asia

Unlike in the past, when you move to Malaysia, you will have the chance to discover Asia in all its glory. Whether by boat trips or short air flights, you can easily afford to explore beautiful Singapore or perhaps spend a relaxing weekend in Bali. The options are endless when it comes to finding incredible vacationing spots around Malaysia. Furthermore, retiring in Asia is a great opportunity for you to experience a new way of living that you would have never had access to otherwise.

• Street Food

It's nearly impossible to talk about Malaysia without mentioning the exquisite selection of street foods that you can enjoy at every corner. The variety of dishes will open your eyes (and palate) to a new life and get you acquainted with the rich culture and flavors of Malaysia.

• Safety

Malaysia is considered politically and economically stable, making it one of the safest countries in the world. You don't need to worry about your family's safety; there, you can only expect to find the peace of mind that you wish for your retirement years.

These are only a few of the benefits that you can expect from your prospective life in Malaysia. As you can see, this versatile country has something for everyone. In the next chapter, we will dig deeper into healthcare in Malaysia since it's not something that you should compromise on when deciding on your retirement destination.

HEALTHCARE IN MALAYSIA

As we mentioned earlier, the developed healthcare system will play a vital role in your decision to retire early in Malaysia. It is no secret to anyone that healthcare can be expensive. In the United States, the inability to pay off medical bills is one of the main reasons behind filing for bankruptcy. Because you can never foretell when and what treatments you might need, you will want to make sure that you always have access to reliable healthcare providers and decent hospitals. While you can compromise on the size of your house or the number of vacations you take annually, the same cannot be said about healthcare. Especially if you will be living away from your home country, you need to feel confident that you and your family have proper medical coverage. There are two types of healthcare systems in Malaysia: public and private. The universal public system is exclusive for Malaysian citizens. However, as a permanent resident, for extra fees, you will be granted access to basic coverage for common illnesses. The Malaysian government has done a commendable job during the last decade in this domain; this is reflected in the quality of the medical staff as well as the healthcare facilities found everywhere in the country. To help you understand how the system works there, here is some important information to keep in mind:

• Public Versus Private Healthcare

Although there is almost no difference when it comes to the quality of medical professionals and equipment, the private sector excels on other fronts. If you or a family member suffers from a health condition that requires close attention and monitoring, you will have a higher chance of getting timely care in a private hospital. Furthermore, private-sector health entities offer higher salaries to their staff, which explains why there is never a shortage of personnel and why the service is generally always faster.

• Highly Trained Medical Staff

In any Malaysian hospital, you will find a good number of professional medical staff who have studied abroad and have undergone international training. As a retiree, it's comforting to know that if/when you need it, you will have access to world-class healthcare providers for a fraction of what you would typically pay back home. It's also worth mentioning that most of the doctors in private hospitals speak English and other major European languages, so there is little to no chance of being misdiagnosed due to mistranslations or poor communication.

• Malaysia Has Become a Hub for Medical Tourism

In recent years, the Malaysian government has been working towards preparing the country to become a destination for medical tourism. And this not only for Malaysian nationals but also for retirees like yourself and other short-term visitors, which may explain the growing number of medical schools across the country and increased funding for the healthcare sector. The unique blend of Western and Eastern medicinal approaches is also one of the main boons Malaysia is relying on to attract curious foreigners interested in new treatments. As such, you can only expect the Malaysian healthcare system to get better and more advanced in the near future. This is excellent news for someone looking to retire early in Malaysia.

• You Will Need to Invest in Private Medical Insurance

Since the country doesn't provide a national insurance program, you will have to invest in a private one yourself. Fortunately, you have a variety of plans to choose from that will cost you a fraction of what you would have to pay back home. Even though compared to what Malaysian nationals are spending for similar services, you are getting more than your money's worth in exchange for the quality of healthcare you are being offered. A doctor's visit at a private clinic can cost as little as 5 USD, which is decidedly cheaper when compared to standard American and European medical fees. Malaysia is not short on medical insurance providers, so you'll definitely find a comprehensive plan that suits your own needs. That said, make sure you select a plan that gives you access to a number of both public and private hospitals.

• HealthCare Screening Packages are Widely Popular

In order to keep up with regular checkups, most Malaysian hospitals offer screening packages that include routine services such as vision tests, bloodwork, and X-rays. These packages come at an average of 70 USD. Interestingly, you have the possibility to add or remove services as per your preference and health requirements. It's yet further proof that the people's wellbeing is at the center of the Malaysian healthcare system.

• Medication is Accessible

Pharmacies are virtually everywhere in Malaysia. You will find that most pharmacists in the country are very knowledgeable and will help you find what you are looking for. You will also be pleasantly surprised to know that medications are relatively more affordable in Malaysia than in Western countries. However, before you plan your move, make sure you have the generic names of your prescription drugs, and not just the brand name to avoid any confusion.

• There is No Waiting Time

Seeing a specialist in Malaysia is as easy as showing up at a hospital and waiting for your turn. Unlike many developed nations, you do not have to wait for weeks, even months, before seeing a doctor for your medical condition. As you grow older, this is the kind of service that you deserve. Thanks to many hospitals and medical facilities, you will never have to worry about booking an appointment for yourself or your spouse to receive treatment.

• Medical Service is Impeccable

The kindness, reliability, and friendliness of the Malaysian people have reflected yet again in their medical services. The national medical staff are professional and show genuine interest in their patients' wellbeing. In most cases, the quality of medical care in Malaysia can only be described as impeccable. You will find it quite easy to find doctors whom you can trust. They will make you feel confident that you are indeed in good hands.

Ultimately, the healthcare system in Malaysia is by far one of the most compelling reasons why this country is a perfect match for retirees. It's also living proof that premium healthcare can be affordable and doesn't have to cost as much as certain nations believe.

HOW TO BE FINANCIALLY INDEPENDENT IN MALAYSIA

After what you have read about the benefits of retiring in Malaysia and how it seems like the ultimate destination, you are probably ready to book your ticket. Nevertheless, there's still a very important variable of the equation that you need to work out before heading East: How do you ensure that you are financially independent throughout your retirement years in Malaysia? How can you guarantee your family's satisfaction, money-wise? This is the key if you want your early retirement plan to work. The principle of early retirement is that you stop working. However, you still need to ensure a decent income to keep you covered. In this chapter, we will be looking at the different options you have as a retiree in Malaysia. Most of the ideas included here are tried and tested by people who have had successful experiences in Malaysia and can rightfully give proper advice. So, if your spouse is still on the fence about this seemingly wild plan, share these few points with them:

Decide on the Retirement Lifestyle You Wish to Have

Before we start discussing the ways that can help prepare you financially for retirement, you need to decide what kind of lifestyle you are seeking. Answering this fundamental question will guide you through the rest of this chapter. Sit with your spouse and imagine the lifestyle that you would deem appropriate for you as a retiree. What do you care about the most? Is it owning a lavish property? Or perhaps you can do without the impressive home but need to have enough money to go on vacation. Almost all of the people who succeeded in early retirement overseas began by defining their goals and objectives for this phase of their lives. Once you have a clear answer to these questions, you can move on to the tips below:

• Live on Less than Your Income

According to retirees who chose to head to Malaysia, living on less than your income is of the essence if you want to ensure you are financially covered. Early on, when establishing some rough estimates about your financial prospects in Malaysia, value your disposable income well below your actual income figure. By doing so, you will give yourself a decent buffer should things ever go south. If your level of income allows you to dine out every day, choose to scale it back to twice or three times a week. The same goes for your vacation planning; instead of traveling back home every year to see your loved ones, promote the fact that you live in Malaysia and encourage them to come to visit for their annual vacations. Some small tweaks will not necessarily impact the lifestyle that you wish for. However, they will end up saving you a considerable amount of money. After all, you will be living in a foreign land away from your direct entourage, so you need all the assurances you can get to provide the necessary support for yourself and your family.

• Diversify Your Investments

Your investment portfolio is more or less the bread and butter of your retirement years. If you still haven't started making lucrative investments, now would be an ideal time to start. You don't have to be a stock market expert to build a solid portfolio. You can meet up with investment bankers and share with them your goal to retire early so that they can help you invest your money safely and efficiently. Choose a combination of monthly paying funds to finance your daily expenses as well as high growth stocks that can pay big annual dividends. The most important thing to keep in mind is to strengthen your portfolio by diversifying your investments as much as possible. This way, you can rest assured that your portfolio is stable enough to carry you comfortably through retirement in Malaysia.

• Keep Your Retirement Savings Account Intact

If you succeed in building a solid investment portfolio, you should be able to avoid dipping into your retirement savings account for quite some time. In essence, retiring early implies that you still have a few years ahead before your retirement account kicks in. It's always handy to have an amount of money set aside for emergencies; in your case, your retirement account can be just that. Discuss possible alternative retirement plans with your current employer to feed your savings account without undermining your disposable income.

• Don't Accumulate Debt

What follows is well beyond debate: If you want to retire early, you need to start making real lifestyle changes today. Debt has no place in an early retirement plan; a 30-year mortgage or a debilitating student loan will only hold you back and prevent you from striking a good financial balance. Even a small credit card debt for unessential items can stall your plans and have you defer your retirement for a couple more years. This is not to say that if you already have debt, you should kiss your early retirement plan in Malaysia goodbye. On the contrary, think of it as a wake-up call to start adjusting your spending behavior and only spend money that you actually have whenever possible. As for your current debts, you should try to find new ways to use any money surplus you have today to settle them. More often than not, something as simple as forgoing your daily cup of to-go coffee can make a world of difference in your account balance come to the end of the month.

• Embrace Minimalism

Luckily for you, riding the current minimalist trend shouldn't be so hard to achieve. Starting with your closet, pull out pieces that you rarely use and sell them online. If you have any valuable items that no longer serve you in any way, sell them to a consignment store and grow your savings accounts instead. You will be surprised at the amount of junk you are needlessly holding on to. Besides, clearing your physical space will positively reflect on your mental state, and you will notice a significant improvement in your overall wellbeing. This is a great way to prepare both financially and psychologically for your time in Malaysia.

• Find a Side Hustle

A few more years of pushing through in the corporate world can be the best thing to do for your early retirement plan. Be smart about utilizing your free time. If you can, try to get a second job or freelance missions to boost your income, hone your skills, and help you pay off your debts to polish your finances for retirement. Remember that your future early retiree self will thank you for any extra work that you take on today!

Being financially independent is a goal of its own right, regardless of where you plan to retire. However, if you have your eyes set in Malaysia, you need to make sure that the numbers you are coming up with will help you achieve the life you wish to live there. Connect with other ex-pats in Malaysia and benefit from their insiders' tips. Even if you are still in the early stages of your plan and still can't afford to take a trip down there, join online groups and forums, and find answers to your important questions.

It's now time for you to learn about some factors that you need to keep in mind before retiring in Malaysia.

FACTORS TO CONSIDER BEFORE MOVING TO MALAYSIA

As we move closer to concluding this journey of discovering early retirement in Malaysia, it is imperative to mention a few aspects you need to look out for. Regardless of the kind of life that you're currently leading, you don't necessarily have to sustain it. In fact, you should be brave enough to reimagine this next phase of your life and seek new thrills and adventures that you never had the time or the money for in the past. Try new sports, eat new foods, and challenge yourself to go out of your comfort zone. After all, you are considering moving halfway across the world during what people deem to be "the final stage." What we mentioned before about the beauty of Malaysia, its excellent healthcare, and amazing people remain true. However, you will still be a foreigner, so it's best to be well-prepared ahead of your journey. Here are some insights that will come in handy:

• Cost of Living

This data is an average of costs across Malaysia in 2020. Prices will differ depending on the city.

ITEM	Malaysian Ringgit	US Dollar	Euro
Rental Apartment (1 bedroom, 1 month) in City Centre	1,502.77 RM	$360.51	€309.77
Rental Apartment (1 bedroom, 1 month) Outside of City Centre	944.42 RM	$226.56	€194.67
Gasoline (1 gallon)	8.02 RM	$1.92	€1.65
Loaf of Fresh White Bread (1 lb)	3.06 RM	$0.73	€0.63
3 Course Meal for 2 People, Mid-range Restaurant	60.00 RM	$14.39	€12.37

Basic Utilities (Electricity, Heating, Cooling, Water, Garbage) for 915 sq ft Apartment	199.87 RM	$47.95	€41.20
1 Pair of Jeans (Levis 501 Or Similar)	221.85 RM	$53.22	€45.73

• Culture and Traditions

Although Malaysia is full of ex-pats inhabiting the tall skyscrapers scattered across the country, it's still considered a rather conservative country. Like most Muslim-majority nations, the work week in Malaysia runs from Sunday through Thursday. Fridays tend to be slow as people usually go out for prayers then spend the rest of the day with their families. In the Malayan culture, foreigners and senior citizens are highly respected, which might be something that would put your mind at ease. You will always be greeted with respect, and the locals will show great enthusiasm in making you feel welcome and appreciated.

You will notice that the locals on the street are dressed modestly; unlike Western societies, overly revealing clothes are uncommon and can, in fact, be offensive to the public. While purging your closet as advised previously, you might want to keep that in mind and start investing in a more suitable wardrobe instead. Choose light, airy fabrics to carry you well during the hot season, which is rather long in Malaysia. As an Islamic nation, Malaysia celebrates the month of Ramadan, where people fast from sunrise until sunset. During that month, you should be careful not to eat in public during fasting hours as a sign of respect for the people. Furthermore, to facilitate your integration as a new resident in Malaysia, it could be a nice gesture to try fasting with your Malaysian neighbors and friends. This will help you better understand the local customs and appreciate the culture. Spend your time ahead of your move reading about the Malaysian culture and study the dos and don'ts to avoid surprises upon your arrival. Malaysia is a multicultural land where locals from different ethnicities live in peace amongst foreigners and tourists, so the people are already very tolerant. Ultimately, your eagerness and openness to learning about your new country of residence will encourage the Malaysian people to welcome you with open arms.

• Acquiring Your Driving License

As a foreigner in Malaysia, you will be allowed to drive using your native license for up to 90 days. Past this period, you will be expected to apply for a local license to avoid being fined. Fuel prices are much lower than in Western countries, so this won't strain your budget. As a former British colony, driving in Malaysia is on the left side of the road. Adding to that, the heavy traffic and motorcycles flying by, navigating can be more challenging than what you are used to backing home. Now, if you are not eager to practice opposite side driving, ex-pats living in Malaysia claim that you can very well do without a car. You may either unleash your adventurous spirit and get yourself a scooter or simply rely on Uber services to get you around for a reasonable fare.

• Taxes are Low

In Malaysia, you will have the opportunity to acquire property at their market value without worrying about hefty taxes. This will make it possible for you to invest in real estate as part of your diversified portfolio that we discussed for your financial independence. The Malaysian government has been intently protecting the value of the Ringgit, the local currency, to keep it competitive in the financial markets. As a result, both nationals and ex-pats living in Malaysia benefit from accessible and affordable public services.

• Getting Your Residency Permit

You will probably want to apply for "Malaysia My Second Home." Those who fulfill the criteria of the program will be offered a renewable 10 years multiple entry social visit pass. This program exists to attract retirees and is the reason why there are so many ex-pats living in Malaysia. http://www.mm2h.gov.my/

• Residential Costs

It's a good idea to start looking for accommodation a few months ahead of your arrival in Malaysia. This way, you will have the time to research different neighborhoods and understand average prices before you can make a final decision. Also, keep in mind that, unlike other countries, rent prices in Malaysia usually don't include utilities like electricity and water expenses. Give yourself the time to ask around and liaise with other ex-pats to understand the pros and cons of different neighborhoods and help you find what you are looking for.

• The Malaysian Government Controls the Internet

While this might be a deal-breaker for some, it's good to keep in mind that the internet in Malaysia is surveilled by the government. As a foreigner, you are advised to use common sense when choosing what to share on your social media platforms. You are preparing this early retirement in Malaysia to enjoy a peaceful life, so always be respectful and avoid putting yourself in difficult situations. By all means, be yourself and speak your mind, but remember that you are still an alien and haven't earned the right to, for example, openly criticize political figures in Malaysia.

• You Will Need a Local Moving Company

Hiring a local moving company to handle shipping your belongings overseas is more advantageous than hiring a foreign one. Make sure the company is legitimate and has registered a trade license in Malaysia to avoid falling victim to malicious scams. Local shipping businesses have the means and know-how to handle custom authorities, which can save you the hassle and any possible delays in retrieving your belongings.

As you would with any other country, it's always recommended to do thorough research before taking the plunge. The aforementioned factors will prove valuable when to picture your life as a retiree in Malaysia. As you can see, there are plenty of things to look forward to, along with tons of adventures waiting for you.

In the upcoming final chapter, we will be giving you some fast, actionable items that you can start with today to help you prepare for your new life in Malaysia.

WHAT CAN YOU DO NOW?

Don't despair if you feel like your move to Malaysia seems elusive at the moment. Here, we give you some actionable items that you can perform right away to guarantee a smooth and safe move. Don't think of the below as extra tasks on your already stacked schedule. Instead, think of it as laying down the foundations for a retirement life full of prosperity and comfort. Without further ado, grab a pen and paper and start taking notes!

• Read All about Life in Malaysia

Just like you would with a college paper, pull out every source you can find, and discover everything you can possibly know about Malaysia. Visit your local library to find books about Malaysia, read online articles and specialized guides, and join ex-pat forums. Even the tiniest detail can help you paint a more accurate picture of life in Malaysia and what to expect once there. Get your spouse excited about the move and start adding some Asian flavors to your daily lives. Try out Malaysian recipes to prepare your palate for your new home. Whatever you can do to get acquainted with the culture and traditions of Malaysia, do it now.

• Book Your Trip

While you might already have read all the books and can probably write a book about Malaysia, this cannot make up for a real visit. As soon as your finances allow it, you should book a trip to Malaysia to get a true feel of what it's like to live there. Plan your visit wisely and don't simply go as a tourist; dedicate enough time and money to tour different cities to be able to decide which ones would best suit your envisioned lifestyle. While you are there, get in touch with local realtors and ask about the rent prices to find out the best time to contact them for getting the property you want. Naturally, the amount of information you will have accumulated throughout your trip can be overwhelming, so make sure to prepare a detailed list beforehand of what you need to do and see in person as opposed to what you can just find online. This way, you will be sure to invest the limited time you have in Malaysia is the best and most productive way.

• Save, Save, Save

Start saving right now. As mentioned earlier, small savings will quickly add up and can easily serve as a cushion for your retirement expenses. A good approach in these situations is to adopt a 'deferred pleasure' mentality in your daily life. For instance, rather than spend a fortune on a family trip to Europe, put it off a few years, and tour Asia instead. Not only will you be able to afford it since it's close by, but you will be in a position where you have minimal responsibilities, which will enable you to enjoy and appreciate your time with your family even more.

Enjoy the Process

The last task we will leave you with is to enjoy the process. Your intention to live frugally is not supposed to make you feel miserable or helpless. As a matter of fact, you should take pride in the fact that while your peers are busy mindlessly squandering their hard-earned cash, you are planning for a future life of abundance and convenience in an exotic land. You will be surprised at how your early retirement plan will give you a sense of purpose and make your work even more meaningful than it already is.

CONCLUSION

Early retirement has never been more popular than in the last few years. Globalization has allowed us to think beyond borders and encouraged us to dream about living in faraway lands. As you have discovered throughout this book, even though Malaysia might sound like worlds away from where you call home, it's more than well-equipped to be your ideal retirement destination. As a retiree your number one concern is understandably healthcare and how you can ensure your family's wellbeing and safety. Hopefully, in Chapter 2, you found compelling evidence that on the healthcare front, Malaysia can offer you the same level of care that you would get at home for a fraction of the price. The Malaysian government is continuing to grow and promote the country as a destination for foreign retirees, so you should be expecting yet more services in the long run. Whenever you are ready to implement serious steps in your early retirement plan, pull out this book, start small with the actionable items in the final chapter, then move onto the more comprehensive items discussed in Chapter 3 to start preparing for your financial independence. This book will provide you with useful tips along every step of your journey. Don't be put-off by your misgivings and embrace the challenges that come along with this exciting adventure that is awaiting you. After all, you will have worked your whole life, and it's now the time to invest in the retirement that you have always dreamed of!

A QUICK NOTE

And finally, if you liked the book, I would like to ask you to do me a favor and leave a review for the book on Amazon. This book is intentionally short so that it fits under the quick read category. Let me know in the review if you want this book to be longer or to include any additional information. Just go to your account on Amazon or type in links below.

http://mybook.to/RetireMalaysia

If you want a free copy of my next book, please sign up to be on my VIP list.

https://www.subscribepage.com/getafreebook

Thank you and good luck!

REFERENCES

-https://blog.pssremovals.com/21-reasons-why-you-should-move-to-malaysia

-https://goexpat.com/top-5-destinations-for-expats-in-malaysia/

-https://www.mm2h.com/16-reasons-to-settle-in-malaysia/

-https://www.aia.com.my/en/what-matters/health-wellness/healthcare-in-malaysia.html

-https://internationalliving.com/countries/malaysia/healthcare-in-malaysia/

-https://www.expat.com/en/guide/asia/malaysia/11902-health-care-in-malaysia.html

-https://www.allianzcare.com/en/support/health-and-wellness/national-healthcare-systems/healthcare-in-malaysia.html

-https://mypf.my/2019/09/27/achieving-financial-independence-the-fi-re-way/

-http://www.expatfinder.com/moving-to-malaysia

-https://www.eurosender.com/en/rr/moving-to/malaysia

-https://asianinspirations.com.au/experiences/10-interesting-malay-customs-and-traditions/